GW01326327

Manipulation & Dark Psychology

Dominate Your Conversation and Analyze People With Proven Methods to Master Body Language, Persuasion & Mind Control, and Develop Effective Communication Skills

Richard Hawkins

2

3

Table of Contents

6

Introduction

Communicating effectively is a skill that takes time and practice for people to truly master. Many of us are not taught how to properly articulate ourselves and engage in conversation that accurately reflects our thoughts and opinions to the other person. This lack of understanding and skills can result in disputes, conflict, miscommunications, hurt feelings, and other side effects of poor communication skills. With proper practice and knowledge, however, these unwanted side effects can be completely avoided.

Learning to effectively communicate takes time and practice, but it can easily be done with enough devotion to your new skill. As you continue to expand on and build your effective communication skills, be sure to take the time to learn the tips and tricks from this book to refine and enhance your skills altogether. These additional skills and pieces of knowledge will ensure that you are able to effectively and successfully communicate with others. They will assist you in learning new tricks and expanding on ones that you may already have a basic understanding of. The more you implement them, the easier communication will become for you.

Effective Communication: Tips & Tricks was written to help you further master your communication skills and communicate with greater success and ease. This guide will help you take your communication skills to the next level, ensuring that you are consistently communicating in a way that is effective. Effective communication exists as a result of many different aspects being respected and honored in the communication process. Effective communication is a combination of clearly articulating yourself, knowing your audience, and using active listening skills. There are also many other steps that can be implemented to further master the art and ensure that you are easily able to effectively communicate with anyone, no matter who they are, how well you know them, or what the nature of your conversation is.

Effective communication is necessary for anyone who desires to engage in proper communication that is free of the many misunderstandings and byproducts of miscommunication that we are regularly impacted by. If you desire to communicate in a way where you are heard and understood, and where your audience also feels heard and understood, it is imperative that you learn and implement these tips and tricks.

If you are ready to learn about what these tips and tricks are, and how you can implement them into your communication skills, then you are ready to begin reading! Remember, take your time and keep things simple and straight forward. Implement each step one at a time for maximum success, and to refrain from becoming overwhelmed with new information and techniques. The easier you make this process, the easier it will be for you to communicate effectively and professionally. And, of course, enjoy!

Chapter 1: Emphasize on Your Skills

Becoming effective at anything you want to do requires you to practice, often. The same goes for learning to communicate effectively. If you want to be successful with communicating effectively and professionally, you need to put a strong emphasis on your communication skills. There are many ways that you can improve on your communication skills, as long as you are interested in investing yourself into your practice.

To give you an idea of where you can practice and where the following tips and tricks from this guide can be practiced going forward, let's explore various areas where practicing communication skills is effective. Since active conversation is already a given, we are going to look at more solutions beyond this basic setting.

Take Communication Classes

Communication classes are available in many communities and are a wonderful resource for those who are looking to put their new skills to use. Communication classes are often lead by teachers, mentors, or coaches who are effectively using communication in their own lives. As a result, they can teach you how to communicate more effectively in your own life as well.

Using communication classes as a means to begin practicing your communication skills provides you with a wonderful opportunity to have active, hands-on guidance during your learning experience. This also gives you the ability to practice with other students who are learning alongside you. For some people, learning at the same time as others makes the process a lot easier. Knowing that you are not practicing on someone who may be judging your skills means that you can eliminate the pressure and truly get some effective practice in. Furthermore, people gather at these classes specifically for the purpose of learning to communicate. This means that there are a lot of incredible tools that you can gain here. As well, because you are practicing directly alongside a teacher, mentor, or coach, you can be given advice based on your specific skillset. If they recognize that you are excelling in one area but may be struggling in another area, for example, they can point this out to you and provide you with information to assist you in improving your skills.

Read as Often as You Can

Reading is another wonderful way to improve your communication skills. When you read, you gain the opportunity to learn more about how other people communicate. Through this process, you can learn about many techniques and practices that are unique to various areas of communication. For example, through actively reading you can quickly pick up on what types of words are regularly used in professional writing, versus that which are used in more casual writing pieces. This will allow you to understand what type of language is typically deemed acceptable in various circumstances. It can also help broaden your vocabulary and assist you in learning how to integrate various words into unique sentence structures.

When it comes to using reading as a tool to assist you in practicing your communication, you want to read as many different forms of written material as you can. Look toward reading newspapers, magazines, fiction and non-fiction novels, blog posts, and more. The more you diversify the materials that you use for this practice, the more you are going to be exposed to a variety of communication styles.

Practice with Other Successful Communicators

Often, learning from those who are already successfully using the skills that you desire to have is a great way to begin growing your own skills. Regularly engaging in conversation with people who communicate at the level you wish to communicate at allows you to actively pick up on their skills and grow your own. When you converse with people who are already communicating at the level you desire to, it becomes easier to see how the various skills are used in practice. It also encourages you to communicate in this way so that you feel more natural and fluent in the conversation you are sharing.

There are many instances where you can find people who are communicating at the level you desire to communicate at. For example, if you intend to communicate professionally, conversing with those who are already conversing on a professional level is a great place to start. You will begin to expand your vocabulary into that unique element, as well as learn how to effectively use those new vocabulary words in active conversation. The same goes for anywhere else. The more we spend time with people who communicate and behave in a way that we desire to, the easier it is for us to integrate those new methods of communication and behavior into our own systems.

Use Your Skills All the Time

Lastly, if you truly want to have success with learning to communicate at a more advanced and effective level, you should be practicing your skills all the time. Those who communicate effectively do not turn their communication skills "on" or "off" from conversation to conversation. This would ultimately result in them not being able to communicate as effectively overall. Instead, they communicate with their new communication skills all of the time. Through regular and consistent practice, it becomes significantly easier to assimilate these new skills into their practice.

You should be using your new conversation skills on a daily basis with anyone you speak with. Whether it is family, friends, cashiers, co-workers, bosses, or otherwise, communicate in the same way on a consistent basis. When you do this, you will gain plenty of opportunity to expand your practice and skills. This will result in you communicating more effectively consistently, and with ease. There will be no considering "how" to communicate between person to person, because you will do it the same way every time: effectively and professionally.

Chapter 2: Keep Things Simple

When we attempt to integrate difficult skills into our communication strategies, it can create a world of distraction and chaos. Trying to recall difficult strategies and integrate them in active practice is challenging, especially when you are likely already communicating beyond your present level of experience. Keeping things simple is necessary if you want to communicate effectively with other people.

When You Don't Simplify

When you attempt to add too many complex strategies and skills in place at any given time, effectively communicating can be challenging. Not only will you struggle to recall the many different strategies you are attempting to integrate, but your audience will also struggle to understand what you are attempting to communicate. There is no need for communication to be a difficult, complex, or over-done process. In fact, the very opposite tends to work far better.

Think about it: if you are trying to learn to communicate more effectively and with greater professionalism, stumbling over your words and taking several moments between sentences to attempt to recall all of your unique strategies will be a struggle. You are likely going to struggle to integrate *any* communication skills because you are attempting to integrate too many to begin with. Furthermore, the majority of people do not communicate at a complex level. Attempting to communicate with your audience with an advanced level of complexity may result in them becoming confused and not thoroughly understanding what it is that you are attempting to say. Most people like things straight forward and to the point. Keeping it clean and simple like this ensures that they know exactly what they are being told and prevents miscommunications from happening. Attempting to interpret too many different, potentially conflicted pieces of communication can become stressful and will result in both you and your audience being out of sync. Chances are, the entire conversation will feel messy and confusing and no one will truly understand what it is that you are trying to accomplish.

Simplifying the process means that you choose the most direct route to get to your point. You keep your words clean, simple, and clear. You directly tell your audience what it is that you are trying to communicate, and you use the best vocabulary to communicate your point perfectly. In doing so, it becomes significantly easier for them to understand what it is that you are trying to express to them. It also prevents you from getting confused in the process of actually trying to express it to begin with. Ultimately, what happens is that the conversation remains clear and consistent, and everyone understands what the purpose of the conversation is.

How Simplification Works

Simplification is actually an incredibly simple process. If it weren't, it would contradict itself! Simplifying your communication skills requires two things: regular practice, and an understanding of how to clearly and directly communicate your piece at any given time.

Regularly practicing means that you will be able to keep your body language and verbal language in agreeance with one another and effectively communicating exactly what it is that you are attempting to say. Because you are regularly practicing, you will also be able to keep your vocabulary broad. This means that you will consistently call on a variety of words to express yourself, allowing your mind to memorize them and you to feel more natural using them in active conversation. This practice comes through every time that you invest in learning how to directly and clearly articulate yourself.

Knowing how to directly and clearly articulate your thoughts and opinions at any given times means that communication becomes significantly simpler. With a broader vocabulary and a clear knowledge around how you can use it to articulate yourself, it becomes easier to know exactly which words will communicate your exact thoughts and feelings. This means that you can tell people exactly what you are thinking and feeling right away, rather than attempting to "get to it" through several lines of unnecessary communication that do not clearly express yourself.

The more you practice communicating, expanding your vocabulary, and actively using larger words that clearly express yourself, the easier it becomes to simplify your communication skills. Then, instead of attempting to recall too many different strategies or skills, you can easily communicate exactly what it is that you are trying to say. Refining your talent so that you can eliminate any unnecessary verbiage or sentences ensures that you are not wasting your time explaining something that is not necessary or relevant to the conversation.

Chapter 3: Be Clear with Your Message

Expanding off of the practice of simplicity, it is important that you are always clear with your message. Before you attempt to articulate yourself to someone else, know exactly what it is that you want to say. Being clear with your message ensures that everything you say is accurate to what you are thinking and feeling. You are able to then express yourself effectively, efficiently, and with professionalism.

Self-Awareness

The first step of truly being able to add clarity to your message is to know exactly what it is that you are trying to say. Understanding your message comes from having a level of self-awareness that allows you to truly comprehend what your message is. For many of us, poor communication skills start from within. When we are unclear about what it is that we are truly feeling or thinking, it becomes significantly harder for us to communicate these feelings and thoughts to other individuals. Learning how to truly decipher the meanings of our thoughts and feelings and how they translate into what we want to share with the other person is important.

When you are communicating with someone, before you share your message, take a moment to think about what it truly is. Often, the initial thoughts or feelings we have may not be clear or in alignment with what it is that we are actually attempting to convey to the other person. For example, in some situations we may be elated that someone has offered us something, but we are not actually wanting to receive the offer, we are simply grateful that it was made. Alternatively, we may hear something and initially become angry, only to later realize we were actually jealous or disappointed and not actually angry. These types of confusions within our own thoughts and feelings can result in us not communicating them effectively with others, because we are not communicating them effectively with ourselves. Taking your time and learning to decipher what it is that you are truly feeling and thinking is the first step in gaining clarity around your message. Once you are clear in what that is, it becomes significantly easier to share that with other people.

Know Your Perspective

In addition to knowing what you are feeling or thinking, you also need to know your perspective. The way that you can find out your perspective is to ask yourself "why" you are feeling or thinking the way that you are. Doing this will allow you to gain some clarity around the feelings and thoughts themselves. This will help you take them from just a thought or a feeling and turn them into an actual message. For example, "I'm angry" becomes, "I am disappointed that you would say something like that to me." This allows us to take the initial reaction or thought toward something and evolve it into a true perspective and message that we can share with the other person.

Knowing your perspective is also rooted in self-awareness. You must be self-aware enough to be able to dig deeper into the initial reactions you have so that you can translate them into a proper message. Taking your time and enforcing these self-awareness practices will ensure that you are clear on what your message is before you even attempt to share it with someone else. Being clear in yourself makes it significantly easier for you to clearly express yourself to someone else.

Express it Clearly

Now that you fully understand your own position toward the subject you are discussing with another person, it is significantly easier for you to clearly express your message in conversation. The key now is to take your time, choose the appropriate words, and communicate yourself in a way that clearly expresses where you are coming from, and why. Clearly sharing your message the first time prevents you from having to repeatedly create supporting statements surrounding your message so that you can provide clarification on the various areas where you did not effectively express yourself.

Being able to clearly express your message assists in warding off unnecessary experiences that coincide with miscommunications. When we do not effectively express ourselves, we may inadvertently put someone in a position where they become defensive or upset by what we have said. We may also create confusion around our message and make it more challenging for our audience to fully understand us. Even if we end up creating clarity in the end, they will have become so confused by the beginning portion of our attempt that it will not be nearly as effective as it could have been had we expressed ourselves properly the first time. So, it is absolutely crucial that you develop clarity in your message before sharing it, and then that you share it directly and clearly.

Chapter 4: Slow Yourself Down

Often, we find ourselves struggling to effectively communicate with others because we are attempting to communicate too quickly. All too often, we communicate by immediately and automatically expressing the first thing that comes to our minds. This is not something that we are taught, but rather it is something that we learn and continue doing because we are not taught a more effective method of communication. This very practice is responsible for us frequently saying the wrong things, expressing ourselves in a way that does not accurately reflect our thoughts, opinions or feelings, or otherwise communicating in a way that lacks clarity and efficiency. When we stop communicating automatically and begin intentionally thinking about how we wish to communicate, it becomes easier for us to express ourselves accurately to what we are actually feeling and thinking.

Give Yourself a Moment to Think

Whenever you are communicating with anyone, always give yourself a moment to think before responding to the other person. This does not need to be a lengthy or drawn out moment, but rather one that will allow you to quickly check over your thoughts and pick the appropriate expressions to share them with the other person. Taking this moment each time we are communicating, especially with important or sensitive topics, enables us to be absolutely certain that we are going to communicate in a way that is appropriate to how we are actually thinking and feeling.

Often, people automatically respond by immediately saying what comes to mind. These thoughts are typically unfiltered and rarely express exactly what we mean. As a result, we end up finding ourselves entering situations where we begin reconsidering the conversation later and wishing we had expressed ourselves differently. This happens because we did not take the time to accurately consider what it was that we wanted to express the first time around. When we slow down mid-conversation and use this as an opportunity to become clear and direct in our communication, the entire nature of the conversation changes. We express ourselves honestly and openly, but with tact and consideration for the others involved in the conversation. As a result, we end up finding ourselves "regretting" our expression significantly less later on because we did so effectively in the first place. Rather than wishing we had done so differently, we know that we can honestly stand behind what we said because it accurately reflected what we wanted to say.

Do Not Feel Pressured to Respond Before You Know

Although you do not want to keep the person you are conversing with waiting for an incredibly long period of time, it is important that you do not feel pressured to respond before you actually know what it is that you want to say. This is why it is important that you take a few moments before answering, or otherwise sharing a thought with someone.

The less pressure you apply to yourself to answer right away, or to take a specific amount of time before answering, the easier it will be for you to take a moment to tune in with yourself and choose an accurate answer. This may take a second, or it may take several seconds. Rarely will it last upward of about 30 seconds. That is, unless you put too much pressure on yourself.

Feeling pressured to answer right away, or to wait a set amount of time before answering, makes it difficult for you to accurately tune in to what you are thinking and discover a way to communicate it. Instead, you want to eliminate the pressure. You are not required to respond immediately, nor are you required to respond after any preset amount of time. Instead, you should respond once you know what the honest thought is that you are thinking and wanting to express.

Early on, this may take a bit longer. Again, this all comes back to self-awareness. If you are already efficient at tuning in and knowing what is running through your mind, it becomes a lot easier for you to express yourself in a shorter amount of time. However, if you are not already practiced with this, it will take you some time to effectively do so. This means that the more you practice being self-aware to become clear on your message, as identified in the previous chapter, the quicker it will be for you to know exactly what that message is and communicate it. This does take practice and experience, so don't worry if your "slowing down" seems particularly slow in the beginning. The more you get used to using this skill, the easier it becomes for you to quickly tune in and express yourself accurately.

Do Not Let This Become Your New Automatic

One of the biggest reasons you want to enforce this practice is to eliminate automatic answering. Automatically responding to someone's expression or question is a surefire way to express yourself in a way that is not entirely accurate to what you are truly thinking or feeling. This is the exact reason why we are pausing to take a moment. So, for that reason, you do not want to let this become your new automatic. Just because you are getting better at tuning in and knowing yourself and your messages does not mean that you can now resume using automatic responses in conversation. This may reflect your current message, but it will quickly grow outdated as you grow and change and the amount of knowledge you carry also grows and changes.

The only part of this that should become automatic is you intentionally pausing for a second to ensure that you know exactly what it is that you are thinking and wanting to say. If you are going to allow anything to become automatic, let it be that. Turning this into a fluent habit rather than a skill that you must remember makes it that much easier for you to tune in, as you do not have to first think about tuning in, then intentionally tune in. Instead, you will automatically tune in and take a moment to determine your thoughts, feelings, and perspective before answering or providing a response to the person you are conversing with.

Chapter 5: Ensure You Are Understood

Many times, miscommunication happens because we are not clearly understood by the person we are communicating with. As clearly as we may feel we have expressed ourselves, the way it is coming across to the other person may not be clear enough for them to truly comprehend what we meant versus what we said. For that reason, it is important that you take the time to ensure that you are actually being understood by the person you are talking to. Giving this extra effort in conversation and in communication in general ensures that no miscommunication takes place to begin with, therefore there is no reason for the byproducts of miscommunication to fester and grow following the conversation.

Ensuring that you have been understood by the person you are communicating with takes some skill, a few easy steps, and a willingness to understand that you may have contributed to the miscommunication if one does occur. You will learn all about this in the following sections.

Communicating Clearly Helps

We have spent the last few chapters getting focused on how you can communicate clearly and to-the-point of exactly what you are thinking and feeling at any given time. You should know that when it comes to avoiding miscommunications and ensuring that the opposing party in the conversation understands you, that these tools will all help. Slowing down and taking the time to master these skills will ensure that you are understood by anyone whom you communicate with. This will help eliminate miscommunications and ensure that you are not exposed to the byproduct of miscommunications, such as anger, frustration, arguments, or inaccurately fulfilled duties by people who misunderstood your requests.

Look for Clues of Understanding

The first thing you should do is look for clues that the person you are communicating with understood you. If a person understood you, there are many signs that they may express. Nodding their head in agreement, having an open and soft body language that is receptive, and looking clearly at you are all good physical clues that the person you are talking to understands what you have said. Furthermore, they should be able to easily relay back to you what it is that you have shared with them. While not every conversation will include the other person repeating back what you said to them, the following responses they provide should clearly align with what you have shared. If they communicate back with you in a way that is very clear to what you have already shared with them and expresses no clear signs of confusion or misunderstanding, there is a good chance that what they have heard and understood is in alignment with what you have said. Other ways to ensure that the person understood what you meant may arise if you have asked a person to do something and they fulfill the duty properly based on the information you have provided them with. If the duty is fulfilled improperly, there is a good chance that the communication between you and them was not clearly articulated.

If someone does not understand what you have said to them, their clues will be completely different. Their heads may be completely still with their eyebrows pinched and a somewhat confused look on their face, expressing that they are not entirely clear on what it is that you are trying to communicate to them. They may cross their arms or grasp at one arm with their opposing hand to show that they are feeling confused and potentially nervous in the conversation. They may also tune out eventually if they feel that they truly are not getting it and that the level of communication is not improving despite them attempting to gain clarity. Verbal cues that they are not fully understanding what you have said include asking several questions to clarify what you meant, as well as providing answers that are not clearly in alignment with what it is that you meant. If the conversation warrants them repeating your message back to you, they will not be able to do so clearly because they will not be sure as to what the message actually was.

It is important that you look for these cues on the person that you are talking to. You want to ensure that you are receiving positive verbal and non-verbal feedback that gives you clear confirmation that the person you are communicating with understands what you are saying. Knowing that the message was communicated appropriately right away ensures that nothing larger grows from the miscommunication that may have taken place during your conversation.

Consider How You Have Contributed to Misunderstandings

When misunderstandings do arise, which they do from time to time no matter how well we attempt to communicate with others, it is important that we look at the situation objectively. Often, we want to quickly jump into a defensive mode and point our fingers at the other person, blaming them for the misunderstanding. It feels easier to blame them for not "getting it" than it is to blame ourselves for the fact that we may have not communicated ourselves clearly enough. Although this may make ourselves feel better in regard to who is to blame, it will not assist us in accurately and effectively clearing up the byproducts of the miscommunication itself.

First off, when we point blame at someone else it results in them also entering a defensive state of mind. This means that the miscommunication will further fester and become a complete argument or conflict between yourself and another individual. Once this occurs, the likelihood that effective and positive communication skills will be applied to this conversation drops significantly. Arguments, defensiveness, and conflict often lead to us communicating poorly as we automatically say what comes to mind as an attempt to deflect the conflict and protect ourselves from feeling hurt or attacked by the other person. When two people enter this state, the conflict becomes harder to resolve, sometimes requiring mediation for positive and effective communication to begin to be used once more.

Second, blaming the other person does not allow us to clearly identify where the communication went wrong to begin with. This is because we have quickly resorted to an argument of trying to identify who is right and who is wrong, rather than an opportunity for effective communication to ensue. As a result, we are not able to learn from the experience and therefore it becomes more likely to happen again at some point in the future.

The reality is, in these scenarios, most often it is both people who are to blame. One person failed to communicate effectively in the first place, and the second person then failed to communicate that they were not completely clear on what was being told to them to begin with. As a result, both have contributed to unclear communication practices, and both have failed to mention that they were unclear to begin with. Then, both parties take their lack of clarity with them and find themselves feeling confused and uncertain about what was gained from the conversation. They may also end up taking hurt and guilt with them from anything that may have come up during the conflict that was shared.

Use This as an Opportunity to Grow Stronger in Your Skills

The best thing you can do is to own your part in the miscommunication and request that the opposing party explain to you how or why they were unclear on what it was that you had attempted to communicate. Using this as an opportunity to clearly pinpoint where the miscommunication began and what caused it is a wonderful opportunity for you to learn how to enhance your communication skills and communicate more effectively going forward.

Even if you are entirely to blame for the conversation resulting in miscommunication and confusion, ask for assistance in understanding why. Even if you felt you communicated clearly and it was the other person who did not explain that they were unclear with what you had said, ask for assistance in understanding why. As well, attempt to recall the conversation in your mind and see if you can pick up any clues that you may have missed in the moment that proved that the other person was not completely certain as to what was being communicated to them.

Once you have done this, you can then take the chance to identify how the conversation could have been handled differently. You can look for new opportunities to search for understanding from the person you are conversing with in the future, as well as develop new skills to avoid any mistakes you may have made that resulted in the confusion or lack of understanding. This will ensure that you grow from the unfortunate situation, rather than it becoming even more frustrating and potentially leading to further miscommunications of the same degree in the future.

Chapter 6: Consider Your Body Language

As you already likely know, your body language plays a major role in how you communicate with other people. Your body language will either support your message, contradict it, or share an entirely different message altogether. If you want to effectively communicate with other people, you need to learn how you can properly consider your body language to ensure that you are communicating properly with the person you are talking to.

How Your Body Language Might Contradict You

Our body language has the potential to contradict us in many ways, and for many reasons. As a result, we may end up inadvertently sending the wrong messages to people during our conversations. Let's explore some examples whereby your body language may result in you not effectively expressing yourself and your message to the person you are communicating with, and why these situations may happen.

Example 1:

Imagine that you are talking to someone important in a business meeting. Your message boasts confidence, particularly because you have somewhat rehearsed it and you know exactly what you need to say to land the deal. However, you are feeling nervous because you have never pitched a deal this big before. For that reason, you are expressing signals of nervousness. You may be fidgeting, shrinking your appearance, or otherwise using body language signals that share with the other person that you are feeling nervous.

In a hopeful world, the person would understand that you may be nervous for pitching to someone as important as them.

What realistically might happen could be drastically different, however. For example, this body language may express to the other person that you are too nervous to handle this scale of business, and therefore you are a liability and not an asset to the business deal itself. Or, they may feel that you are being dishonest or talking a bigger game than you can actually play because you are too nervous to remain confident during what they may see as a "basic conversation."

As you can see, despite the fact that your verbal language was communicating confidence and poise, your nonverbal language was communicating fear and nervousness. As a result, the person you were communicating with became confused by your message and began picking up on the fact that you may not be the best person for them to work with. Then, no matter how qualified you are for the opportunity, you may miss out because your body language contradicted your message.

Example 2:

Imagine you are meeting with someone in regard to a new job and you are feeling extremely desperate for the meeting to go well. For that reason, you are attempting to maintain a confident and poised appearance as you communicate with that person. Verbally, you may be expressing yourself in a confident way. However, your clenched fists and tight posture may express otherwise.

These body language signs may be showing that you are an angry, aggressive, or particularly anxious person who is not entirely in control of their feelings. Because your emotions are being felt on a physical level and you are not able to physically contain them, they may become fearful of your ability to control yourself in future situations. As a result, the person may not trust you to be able to fulfill your duty because you are overly expressive on an emotional level. You may miss out on the important job position because you are simply too emotional and aggressive to be able to handle the position in the eyes of the interviewer.

Example 3:

Imagine that you are with your romantic partner and you are sharing a romantic night together. However, before the night commenced, you had dealt with a poor day at work and you were feeling torn down and defeated. Although you tell your partner that you are happy to be with them that evening for a romantic time, they are feeling as though you are withdrawn and are questioning whether or not you actually want to be with them that night. For that reason, they may not feel particularly close with you in the moment because they feel like you are holding back. In reality, you are simply feeling defeated and so your body language is slow and not as receptive or romantic as you may normally be.

In this circumstance, your partner may feel worried that something is wrong or that you are not happy with them for some reason, when this is not true at all. Learning to use your body language to effectively communicate your feelings or using your language to effectively communicate why your body language is contradicting your words means that you can convey the truth to your partner. This can prevent them from feeling rejected or otherwise pushed away on what is meant to be a romantic night enjoyed together.

As you can see, when your body language and verbal messages contradict one another, it can be difficult for people to truly believe what you are saying. They may take this as a sign that you are lying, or that you are incompetent for what it is that you are offering. For that reason, you may miss out on opportunities, find yourself or someone else ending up with hurt feelings, or otherwise find strange and unwanted outcomes coming from your conversations. This would not be because your message is off, but rather because you are not supporting your message with the appropriate form of body language.

How to Check in with Your Body Language

When it comes to communicating and recognizing other people's body language, it is quite simple. You regard the other person, watch their movements as they speak and in response to your communication, and you can typically easily tell exactly what they are thinking or feeling as a result. With ourselves, however, it is not as simple. We cannot actually see our own bodies when we are communicating, therefore we may be carrying ourselves in a way that unintentionally says the wrong thing to the person we are talking to. This results in them getting the wrong message from us.

So, that means that we need to learn to check in with our bodies and make sure that we are nonverbally communicating a message that agrees with the message that we are verbally communicating! Once you know how, this becomes simple.

The first step comes with developing a basic awareness and understanding as to what different body language signals mean. After you have an understanding of these meanings, you can then begin doing what is known as a "body scan" on yourself during conversations. This is a quick scan we do to become aware of how we are presently carrying ourselves. It does not take more than a few seconds, and it is heavily important to us being able to check our body language and adjust accordingly. Simply become self-aware over how you are carrying yourself and take a moment to notice where you may be physically communicating in a way that does not align with what you are verbally communicating.

"Speak" In Accordance with Your Words

After you have effectively scanned your body, it is time to adjust your body language to ensure that you are speaking in accordance with your words. This is simple: all you need to do is consider what your message is and choose body language that will effectively communicate your message.

Most of us communicate subconsciously with body language. If we carry feelings in our subconscious, or if we have underlying feelings that we are carrying that are not necessarily relevant to the conversation, we may find that we carry ourselves subconsciously in a way that reflects those feelings rather than in a way that reflects how we feel during the conversation itself. As a result, we miscommunicate. So, it is important that you consciously choose body language signals that will accurately reflect how you are feeling toward the person you are communicating with, and in reference to the message you are communicating. Learning to align these two elements of communication effectively will ensure that you are staying in agreement with what you are actually feeling.

Keep It Fluent

It is important that you stay fluent in your body language. You don't want to be awkwardly, expressively, and obviously adjusting your body language as this will come across as tacky and uncomfortable to the other person. They will be able to sense that your body language is forced and, as a result, they will still feel uncomfortable and uncertain about what it is that you are trying to communicate. They may feel that you are lying or otherwise not being clear, therefore they may become suspicious about you and your intentions.

Ideally, you want to fluidly move through your body language signals and easily express various types of body language. You can do this by practicing in the mirror first, and then taking your skills to the real world by practicing in conversation. It should not look like you are intentionally monitoring and manipulating your body language, even when you actually are. No matter how manufactured your body language may be to match your message, it should still look natural and comfortable. Keeping it fluent and comfortable will ensure that your audience does not become confused, uncomfortable, or suspicious as to why you look so awkward and uncomfortable in your own movements. Since body language *is* something we subconsciously do, looking as though you are consciously monitoring it is strange and often communicates the wrong message to your audience.

Chapter 7: Recognize Who Your Audience Is

When it comes to communicating, how you will adjust your communication styles will heavily depend on who your audience is. Various audiences will communicate in different manners. This means that they will also be receptive to information in different ways. In order to truly communicate in a highly effective manner that allows you to get your message across and refrain from experiencing any confusion or miscommunication, you need to take the time to identify unique audience types.

How Audiences Differ

Audiences differ in many different ways. The easiest way to determine who your audience is begins by determining what category they're in, and then by discovering what tone they operate with. This will give you the best way to understand who your audience truly is. Once you know these two pieces of information, your communication can be adjusted accordingly.

Categories

The categories that audiences fall into are as follows: family, friends, acquaintances, strangers, and professional. These classify the types of people that you are talking to.

Family and friends are people who you are close to and who you already have a strong understanding of. You know these people well, so understanding how they communicate and the basic differences between them and others is simple for you. This may differ, however, if it is a family member that you are not particularly close with or that you regularly find yourself in conflict with. For these individuals, the communication style may be more rigid and uncomfortable by nature.

Acquaintances and strangers are people that you know very little about and therefore it can be difficult to determine how to communicate with them in a way that is most effective at times. Some are easy to read and understand right away, whereas others may be a little more evasive and difficult to interpret.

Professional contacts are ones where the communication style needs to be more intentional and appropriate for professional circumstances. Regardless of what tone the individual has, you need to be wary not to grow too "casual" with these individuals. These relationships and, therefore, communication styles should remain professional at all times.

Tones

Tones are also highly important to pay attention to. These will give you an idea as to how the person communicates. When you are communicating with someone, pay attention to see what their tone is like when they communicate. This will provide you with a vast amount of information in regard to how you can best communicate with this person to prevent confusion or miscommunications. The tones include: casual, aggressive, anxious, professional, and joyful.

Individuals with casual tones are easier to be relaxed around. While you still need to maintain effective communication, you can get away with more relaxed communication styles. This includes joking, and otherwise playing around. You can also refrain from being overly cautious about the topics of conversation, with reason to the person with whom you are conversing with.

An aggressive tone is held by someone who tends to be very forthcoming and, well, aggressive in their communication. They may be very quick to point fingers, very demeaning, and otherwise difficult to communicate with. They have a tendency to be very demanding and uncomfortable to talk to, therefore it is important that you stay very clear and firm in your communication with them. They easily misinterpret things and quickly become enraged by seemingly small things, or their misinterpretations.

Anxious individuals are those who have a tendency to feel very uncomfortable in conversation and will likely be quick to feel awkward. They may frequently show signs of wanting to leave or get away from the conversation. When communicating with them, you need to be very clear and open about what you are saying to prevent them from building up confusions in their mind based on their own anxieties and insecurities.

Professional individuals are very organized. They communicate in an incredibly proper manner with a wide vocabulary. They are direct and clear in their messages and intentions, and they will always ensure that the conversation stays professional. They tend to stay away from "taboo" or uncomfortable subjects, do not like to talk about anything they may deem "unnecessary," and are very conscientious about their time and how it is spent.

Joyful individuals are happy and uplifting. They like to talk to others who are communicating in the same format. They operate best around other individuals who are also uplifting and who can match their high energy. As well, they prefer to keep the topics light and positive, and shy away from gossip and other negative topics that may bring their energy down.

Connecting the Two

When you are communicating with someone, you can determine exactly who your audience is by first locating their category, and then identifying their tone. Once you have identified these two pieces of information, you can then determine what the best way to communicate with them is.

Remember, for maximum growth in your own effective communication skills, it is best if you continue to implement effective practices at all times. Even if you are communicating with a friend who falls under the casual category, you should still continue to practice your effective communication skills. This will ensure that they become habitual and that you have an easier time implementing them on an ongoing basis when it comes to truly matter, such as when you are communicating with professionals who also have a professional tone.

Chapter 8: Use Appropriate Styles of Communication

When you are communicating, it is necessary that you use appropriate styles of communication to ensure that you are being properly received by your audience. Using appropriate styles of communication will ensure that you are able to effectively share what you are thinking and feeling without miscommunications taking place. It also means that you will be able to communicate in a way that your audience can easily receive. You do not want to be communicating in the wrong style and tone for your audience, or you may disrupt your effective communication patterns and find yourself being overtaken by misunderstandings.

Learning to communicate appropriately requires you to identify your audience, communicate in alignment with them, use appropriate vocabulary, and stay on the side of caution whenever necessary. If you implement these strategies, then you will be able to easily communicate in accordance with the audience you are talking to.

Communicating in Alignment with Your Audience

In the previous chapter you learned to identify your audience. Now, it is important that you understand how you can communicate in alignment with your audience. Although this may seem straight forward, there are some "rules" that come into play when it comes to using these categories and tones to determine how you will effectively and appropriately communicate with your audience. The rules are as follows.

Appropriate Subject Matter

The first thing you must consider is that you are communicating with appropriate subject matter. For example, what you joke about with your friends may not be appropriate to joke about with your family or colleagues. This varies from group to group, but also from individual to individual. Some people in your family may be easier to joke with about certain subjects, whereas others may prefer to stay more "safe" in their subject matter. This applies to all categories.

It is important that you honor the receptiveness of your audience and choose subject matter that will be respectful to them. You do not want to be using inappropriate or unacceptable subject matter to communicate with people or you will end up destroying your effective communication strategies. For some people, talking about subject matter that they deem to be "inappropriate" can be highly disrespectful. It is important that you do not cross this line, as you will deplete their receptiveness and put them into a defensive mode. This will result in all further communication being awkward and uncomfortable.

Adjusting Tone Based on Category, Not Tone

The next rule applies primarily to people who fall into the professional category, though it may cross into other categories depending on the unique circumstances. This rule essentially means that, regardless of the tone that the other person may be carrying, you should always respect them for who they are. So, say your boss is a very casual person who generally likes to joke and may sometimes head into more taboo jokes. They may be open and receptive to jokes, and a generally happy and outgoing person. This is wonderful, and typically means good things for you work-wise. However, you should not forget that you *are* communicating with your boss, whom is a part of the professional category. Therefore, you should keep all of your communication professional. While you can still joke and meet their casual and joyful tones, mind your subject matter and use their category as the primary "determining factor" for how you will communicate with them, not their tone.

Vocabulary Choices

Who you are talking to heavily influences how you should verbalize your thoughts and feelings. People from different categories, cultures, backgrounds, and societal classes will all have different preferred vocabulary words. They will communicate differently and, therefore, you need to be able to match their communication styles. This does not necessarily mean that you should "dumb yourself down" for those who do not typically speak in a professional or educated manner. Rather, it means that you should refrain from using words that they likely won't know. This can result in them feeling uncomfortable and potentially intimidated because they are unclear as to what you are saying and therefore they are not entirely certain on how they should be responding.

The same goes with professionals. People in the professional field tend to speak with larger vocabulary words and use a highly educated level of vocabulary in general. For that reason, you want to match their vocabulary by also using higher levels of vocabulary.

The primary reason for adjusting your vocabulary is so that you can effectively communicate your thoughts, opinions, and feelings to your audience in a way that they will understand. If you use vocabulary words that they are not entirely clear on, you are much more likely to find yourself in a position whereby your audience simply does not understand what you are saying. This can lead to miscommunications, misinterpretations, and sometimes a level of defensiveness because they may feel intimidated by you. The best way to avoid this is to communicate on the same level as your audience by using appropriate vocabulary words.

References

In addition to vocabulary words, consider your references when you are communicating with other people. Regularly referring to references that your audience is not likely to understand is not an effective method of communication. In fact, it may lead to disconnects if they truly do not understand what it is that you are referring to, exactly. It is important that you choose references that your audience is likely to understand or know about. This will ensure that they are relatable to your audience and that they understand what you are insinuating when you use these references.

On the Side of Caution

Whenever you are unsure as to how you should be speaking to your audience, always choose to air on the side of caution. Take it slow, and let your audience lead the way by allowing them to show you their tone, express their vocabulary, and choose references that they would understand. This will ensure that you can easily match their communication style and effectively communicate in a way that they understand. That way, there will be no room for miscommunications or misinterpretations!

Chapter 9: Learn to Listen

A large part of communication, a part that we often forget about, is listening. Learning to listen effectively is a good way to ensure that you are communicating effectively, too. Listening provides you with many keys, pieces of information, and clues on how you should be communicating with a person. You can learn a lot by listening, so it is imperative that you learn to effectively listen so that you can effectively communicate with your audience at any given time.

Listen for Clues and Information

When you listen to your audience, they will provide you with many different clues and pieces of information that can help you communicate more effectively. These clues and pieces of information can teach you everything from what their concerns and interests are, to what they like to talk about and how they like to communicate. You can easily learn anything you need to know just by listening to a person talk. If they are not telling you what you need to know, ask the appropriate questions and then honestly listen for the answer.

Listening for what the person is telling you is the best way to get honest and accurate information in the moment. This means that you can learn about what they are most concerned about, interested in, and otherwise passionate about. Then, you can use this information to determine how you are going to effectively communicate back with them.

For example, say that you are talking to an employee of your company who is having a conflict with another employee. If you did not listen, you would not know who the other employee was, what the nature of the conflict was, why it was an issue, or any other pieces of important information that your audience would be providing you with. This means that you would not be able to address the problem effectively, and your audience will not feel heard, or as though you are properly addressing the situation. So, they may grow more frustrated. If, however, you were to listen, you would hear all of the information that you need to know. Then, you could honestly communicate back with your audience and together come up with adequate solutions that would resolve the issue. Your audience would feel appreciated and respected because they have been listened to, and the problem will be resolved in a way that honors both parties. Then, the resolve will be more sustainable and likely to last.

When we listen, our audience tells us everything that we need to know in order to communicate with them effectively. If we ignore them, we are not going to be able to communicate in an appropriate way. We will ultimately fail to understand what they are talking about or how we can connect with them, and our attempts at communication will not meet them with where they are at. As a result, they will feel unappreciated, unheard, and frustrated as a result of ineffective communication.

Listen for Tone

Your audience has their own tone, if you will recall. It is important that you listen to this tone. In addition to clues from their vocabulary, their tone will also provide you with information. Say, for example, a generally upbeat and joyful person suddenly becomes aggressive. This would show you that they are extremely upset with something and that they are feeling heavily conflicted by it. Through properly listening to their tone *and* the information that they are sharing with you, you can easily begin communicating on their level and bring them back down from their changed tones. This is one of the best ways to manage conflict resolutions, as well as to communicate in a way that your audience will be receptive to.

Listen So Your Audience Feels Heard

Lastly, listening is not just for you. This is not just an opportunity for you to hear the clues and pieces of information they give you and identify their tones. It is also an important part of the process for your audience. When we do not allow our audience to feel heard and respected, they will quickly begin to feel unappreciated and disrespected. As a result, they will likely become defensive, frustrated, and even closed. This results in them not wanting to communicate with us any further. They become more susceptible to misinterpreting what we share, less likely to want to share with us in the first place, and less likely to hear what we have to say. This means that the lines of communication are severed, and it will require appropriate effort to allow them to be reopened.

If you are in a position where you cannot effectively listen to your audience, it is important that you clarify this upon the start of the conversation. This way, they feel like you are respecting them, that you appreciate them, and that you honor their need to be heard, but that you are not presently able to give them the required attention to do so. Then, if they want to, they can choose to come talk to you later, or to continue talking to you knowing that you are not able to provide them your undivided attention.

Listening appropriately is highly necessary in allowing your audience to feel heard, respected, appreciated, and honored. If you want to have great success in effective communication with your audience, you need to listen to them as effectively as you would like for them to listen to you. This will make them more receptive to what you have to say and will make them feel like they are a genuine part of the conversation, because they are.

Chapter 10: Mind Your Emotional Tone

The way you convey yourself emotionally plays a large role in how other people interpret what you are saying. If you want to communicate effectively, you need to understand how your emotional tone affects the people that you are communicating with. The key factors to recall when you are communicating with other people is that you need to maintain a positive tone, express empathy effectively, refrain from attacking them or from becoming defensive, and stay friendly. When you enforce these tones, you make yourself open and receptive to your audience. This makes them feel more comfortable and welcomed in your presence, meaning that they will have an easier time communicating with you, too.

Express Empathy

When you are communicating with people, it is always important that you take the time to express empathy. People are far more receptive and open to people who are able to easily express empathy toward other people and their experiences. When you express empathy to your audience, you create an opportunity for them to feel appreciated and respected. When people feel this way in your presence, they are far more likely to feel engaged in conversation with you. This means that not only will they be more receptive to the information that you share, but that they will also be more forgiving if you make a mistake or share it in a way that is not as clear or direct as it could have been. This is also an important part of listening, as we discussed in the previous chapter.

Expressing empathy does not have to be hard, nor does it require a significant amount of energy. It simply requires you to be kind and caring toward their needs, concerns, interests, and hardships. If someone expresses that something was difficult for them, express empathy for the difficulty that they faced. Do this for any emotional experience that they express. This ensures that they feel like you truly understand what they are saying and allows them to feel supported by you.

Be Positive

It is always important to ensure that you stay positive when you are communicating with people. Refrain from complaining, gossiping, or otherwise indulging in pessimistic behaviors when you are communicating with other people. This type of behavior, even if it is being displayed by the other person, completely lowers the energy of the conversation. It can get your audience stuck in their head and feeling absorbed by their own perceived problems and prevent them from completely listening to what you are saying. In other words, it diminishes their receptivity.

Being positive, searching for the silver lining, and staying optimistic in difficult situations or conversations ensures that everyone stays in a high energy mood that serves the conversation. People are more likely to be drawn to you for your positive energy, and they will want to communicate with you more frequently. This is a clear sign of effective communication. In addition to drawing people in toward you, positive communication also keeps people open and receptive. When people are happy, they are more likely to be actively engaged in the conversation and listening to you.

Do Not Attack or Become Defensive

It is important that, no matter what the circumstances are, you refrain from attacking your audience or becoming defensive against them. These two actions, although opposite of one another, immediately close the doors for open communication. They take away any opportunity to have effective communication and leave you both feeling unhappy and like you have been a part of an overtaxing conversation.

Staying objective, even in the face of conflict, is the best way to ensure that you remain clear on what your message is and that you stay focused on effective communication. If the other person becomes defensive or starts attacking, you remaining objective means that you can search for opportunities to continue to carry on lines of effective communication until the conversation can reasonably or naturally come to a close.

In the face of conflict, you should never be the person that drops into negative or unkind behaviors. This will only close off your audience and damage your ability to effectively communicate with them in the future. It will also not solve the conflict but will worsen it altogether. If you want to solve the conflict and have successful communication, you need to set your feelings aside and remain objective, open, and effective in the conversation.

Be Friendly

Being friendly and charismatic is important. Show genuine interest when you are talking to people. Ask them how they are doing, and how their day is going. If it is appropriate to the situation and the relationship, ask about how their family is doing and go into more personal communications. When you are communicating, building friendships and relationships through communication is a great way to open your audience up and increase the ability for you to share effective communication. When people care for us and feel endeared by us, they are more likely to stay engaged in the conversation. They hear what we have to say, they listen to us, and they trust that we will hear them and listen to them. This keeps everything open and easy flowing between you and your audience.

This relationship-building practice does not need to be reserved for those who you know have the potential to have a relationship or friendship with you in the future. You can use these friendly tactics on anyone, from strangers to professionals. Being friendly does not require you to have some form of permanent relationship with the individual that you are being friendly with. It simply opens you up, shows that you are receptive, and provides a warm playing field for communication to exist on. When you are open, receptive, and warm, your audience will be, too. This means that any communication that takes place between you, shallow or deep, meaningful or casual, will be positive.

Conclusion

Effective communication is a skill that many of us do not naturally have because we have never truly been taught about what it means. We often pick up on our communication skills from our interactions with society, and in many cases, these are not the most effective skills to hone. They tend to be riddled with accidental techniques that result in us causing our audience to tune out and feel unreceptive to what we are saying. They can also prevent us from accurately articulating our thoughts and feelings the first time around, without requiring several clarifications to get our point across.

When you properly practice the art of effective communication, you manage to bypass all of these unwanted side effects and communicate effectively with anyone you are talking to. Whether they are receptive or not, you can begin to implement the proper techniques to assist them in clearly understanding you, and to ensure that you are being honest and open with your true message.

I hope that *Effective Communication: Tips & Tricks* was able to assist you in effectively learning communication skills. From assisting you in discovering times to practice, to helping you understand your audience and speak appropriately to their receptivity, I hope that you were able to acquire adequate information to effectively communicate with anyone.

These skills take time and practice, so be sure to go easy on yourself and allow yourself the opportunity to implement them in a way that will be effective for you. Attempting to implement too many new techniques at once or trying to over complicate the situation will result in you not being able to effectively communicate at all. It will likely result in your message becoming confusing, and your audience not truly understanding what it is that you are trying to say. Even if you do manage to finally get it across, they will likely already be too confused from everything you mentioned beforehand to actually get what you mean. The delivery will be ineffective and, therefore, the entire method of communication becomes ineffective. Communication is most effective when it is delivered directly and clearly.

The next step for you is to begin implementing these tricks and tips and learning how they can assist you in effectively communicating with anyone. Be sure to use your new skills at all times to ensure that you maximize your practice and that you get the most out of it. Trying to "switch" between effective and ineffective communication based on your audience will only result in ineffective results. If you want to be effective with communication, you need to dedicate to being effective all of the time.

Lastly, if you enjoyed this book and felt that it assisted you in learning about effective communication, please take the time to rate it on Amazon Kindle. Your honest feedback would be greatly appreciated.

Introduction

Congratulations on downloading this book and thank you for doing so.

Many people look for ways to improve their social life. However, they do not know the specific actions that they should take. Indeed, improving one's social life takes more than having desire; it also has to be accompanied by positive actions. The following chapters will teach you the best techniques that will enrich your social life:

Chapter 1 teaches how you can effectively enrich your social life.

Chapter 2 reveals powerful strategies that you can use to improve and grow your social circle.

Chapter 3 lays down the best practices that you should observe to increase your chances of success.

There are plenty of books on this subject on the market, thanks again for choosing this one! Every effort was made to ensure it is full of as much useful information as possible. Please enjoy!

Chapter 11: Enrich Your Social Life

Build Good Relationships and Be More Connected

The key to a happy and fulfilling social life is to build good relationships with nice and interesting people. But, how do you build good relationships? Indeed, many people want to have meaningful relationships and yet they often end up disappointed. You should understand that building good relationships takes time and effort. More importantly, it takes positive actions. When it comes to taking positive actions, you definitely have so many options. In order not to waste your time, you need only to apply the best techniques that have been proven to be effective means to establish a strong relationship. By the time you finish reading this book, you will be equipped with the best techniques that will turn you into a social magnet.

The main focus of social living is on building good relationships. Remember, though, that the personality of different people also varies. When you socialize with people, you should be ready to meet nice and interesting people, as well as those who are completely arrogant and narcissistic. Do not worry, you do not have to deal with negative people for so long. To have a happy and enjoyable social life, you should not just welcome anybody into your circle. Rather, you should exercise the right to choose who will be included in your inner circle. Your inner circle is composed of the people who are intimately close to you. They are, in layman's term, your closest friends. However, it should be noted that social life means more than the scope of your immediate circle. It includes all the people in your life, especially those with whom you have a relationship with, such as your family, friends, colleagues, and others. Simply put, it refers to the people in your life.

Building good relationships is a mutual process. After all, you cannot force anyone to befriend you. However, there are techniques that you can do to attract and draw people and make them want to connect with you. While there are people who simply hope and wait for luck to happen, those who understand how socializing works know that you can use effective techniques that can significantly increase your chances of having a good relationship. However, do not consider this as a way to manipulate people and make them do what you want. Rather, consider it as a way of improving yourself as a person.

A relationship is created when people connect. A *good* relationship is formed when people connect and like each other. Since your goal is to make good relationships, then you must make yourself likable. Otherwise, people might perceive you as arrogant or disrespectful. If this happens, then chances are that they will stay away from you. The techniques in this book will guide and teach you just how to make yourself likable. In fact, you do not really apply the techniques to become likable. Instead, the techniques in this book should be considered as suggestions of self-development. By developing yourself, people will perceive you as someone they like. This is not about pleasing other people. Rather, people are pleased simply because of who you are. As mentioned in the previous book in the series, sincerity plays an important role in building a good and meaningful social life. Without sincerity, people may find it hard to trust you. Without sincerity, even the good relationships that you have already formed can easily be broken. So, how do you connect and make good relationships? You should improve yourself. And how do you improve yourself? Well, this is the tricky part as there are many ways to go about it. However, rest assured that the techniques in this book could serve as your guiding light to self-development.

The quality of your relationships with people has a big impact on your level of happiness. Studies show that people who have good relationships are often more content and happier with their life, while those who fail to establish good relationships with others often have a high level of stress, and some of them even reach a state of depression. If you want to have a good and happy life, then it is important that you improve your social circle and create meaningful bonds with good people. As the saying goes, "Happiness is only real when shared."

The Social Process

The entire social process is nothing but full of interactions with people. It has a beginning, middle, and end. For as long as you exist in this world, then this social process in your life goes on and on. There is simply no way to escape the reality that you are connected to people except, perhaps, if you abandon everything and go to the wilderness — which is probably not applicable to your life. Now, there are techniques or strategies that you can use throughout this process. These techniques, as revealed in this book, will help create a good relationship and even develop it.

Although the social process may be viewed as something so simple since you will only have to connect and interact with people, it is actually much more than that. Keep in mind that when you socialize, small things matter. Take, for example, the use of eye contact. This is a very simple technique, and yet it can create a big difference. Of course, there are many other things that you can do. The key is to keep yourself and those whom you like in this social process. Hence, this involves continuous connections and interactions, but which do not need to be on a regular basis. The important thing is to keep people in your circle and even expand your social circle by adding more interesting people. This is the social process. It is the process of connecting and interacting. Once you experience it, you will realize that social process means more than just being with people. Rather, it is a way to enjoy life with other people. After all, life is an adventure, and you do not need to travel alone. From time to time, it is fun and good to stop for a while and enjoy the beauty of being alive with others.

On the Use of Social Techniques

It is noteworthy that the use of techniques is not a way to control or manipulate people. Rather, your purpose for learning the techniques should be to improve yourself as a person. Now, it is not easy to break a habit, and it is even harder to replace a bad habit with a positive habit. But, this is doable — and you can do it. When you learn and use the techniques in this book, do not be discouraged if you are not able to execute them effectively in the first few tries. Just keep on practicing them. It is important that you give yourself time to adjust. After a few weeks or months, the more you will get used to these techniques. Soon enough, they will become a natural part of you.

This book divides the strategies that you can use into three: short-term strategies, mid-term strategies, and long-term strategies. Now, take note that these strategies are cumulative. Just because you have reached the mid-term strategies does not mean that you no longer have to apply the previous strategies. In fact, if you can, then you should apply all the strategies at once. However, it should be noted that techniques alone cannot create a meaningful relationship. They can only help you. Consider them as useful tools that you can use. Still, it is important for you to have a good heart and treat people nicely. After all, you do not go out there to use people. This book is not about manipulating others but about making good and sincere relationships. As the saying goes: "Do unto others as you would have them do unto you."

Now, do not think that making good relationships is a big challenge. In fact, the way to it is usually composed of small stuff, but which are usually ignored or neglected. It is up to you to pay attention to these small details and apply them in your everyday dealings. Indeed, every interaction that you make with another person is an opportunity to expand your social circle or further develop an existing relationship. Remember not to take anything and anyone for granted and make every moment count.

The following strategies will help you form new relationships and even develop existing relationships. Be sure to read the explanations carefully for you to realize the value or meaning of every strategy. Again, this is not about manipulating or unduly controlling people. Rather, this is about having more realizations and improving yourself as a person.

Chapter 12: Powerful Strategies

Short-Term Strategies

• Be approachable

A good way to start and invite new relationships into your life is by being approachable. Now, many people are well aware of this. However, a common mistake is simply to say that you will be approachable. This does not create any difference. Realize that to be approachable is not just a decision that you make, but it must also be accompanied by positive and relevant actions. This would include taking the initiative to connect with people. If you have built any walls around you that discourage people from connecting with you, then now is that time for you to bring down those walls and start reaching out to people. Yes, be the one to reach out. You do not have to wait for people to come to you. When people feel or know that you are reaching out to them, the more they will want to connect with you. Do not make it difficult to talk with you. If you want to be approachable, then you should be ready to give your time to people.

When you open your heart and welcome people into your life, you should expect to meet different kinds of people. Some people that come to you may be good and kind while others can be difficult to deal with. This is part of socializing. You will get to meet different kinds of people. To be approachable means that you should not judge people. As another saying goes: "Judge and you will not be judged." How can you expect people to approach you if they feel that you will judge them? A common mistake is to tell people that you are not judging them but then you talk about other people in a negative way. Never say bad things about other people. If you will say something negative, then tell it straight to the person concerned and avoid spreading any gossip. It will also make you less approachable as the other person will think that you might also talk about him badly in the future.

Being approachable is only at the beginning of the social process. It merely invites people into your life and draws them to you. It is still up to you to handle the interaction effectively to lead it into a good relationship. The more approachable you are, the more people you will meet. Although not all of these people will be as nice as you would have them, you will most likely encounter some disappointments. However, this is also the way that will allow you to meet the kind of people that you like. Indeed, there is a risk, but there is also a wonderful reward.

There are people who tend to push others away without realizing it. Observe yourself and be honest. Is there something about you or that makes it difficult to connect with you? For example, being rude or offensive tends to push people away so you should avoid such qualities. A good advice is to fill yourself with positive qualities, such as love, understanding, harmony, and peace.

- Be open and connect

One's social life can be greatly improved simply by being open and connecting with people. Being open means more than allowing people to enter into your life. It also means being open to any conversation with anyone. Just because you are not interested in a certain topic does not mean that you cannot carry a good conversation with another. Do not underestimate the power of listening.

Being open also means taking the initiative. For example, learn to greet people with a smile. Do not forget the simple things like saying "good morning" or "good afternoon." When people talk to you, then stop whatever you are doing and give him your full attention. By being open, you invite more people into your life.

Connecting with people is another thing that you should focus on. The key is to develop or improve whatever connection that you have. The key to doing this is using effective communication. Do not be satisfied with shallow talks. Instead, try to connect with people on a more intimate level. This may not always work as you will meet those who would not remove their walls. However, you will also encounter those with whom a mutual relationship can be made. This usually refers to people who may be included in your inner circle.

The more connected you are to another, the more the relationship develops. As a short-term strategy, connecting simply means having a free-flow of conversation with another. This is easy if you share the same interest with a person as it can be a good topic in conversation. However, what if you do not share the same interest? Is a strong connection still possible? The answer is *yes*. Again, do not underestimate the power of listening. Indeed, there are so many people out there who simply want to have a friend who would listen to them. There are those who do not really want a solution to their problem – they only want to have someone who would understand, or at least try to understand them.

There are many factors that are involved when you use the word, "connection." Now, all these little factors add up to the experience. How you feel about a person and how the other person feels about you matter and usually depend on how strong the connection is. It is worth noting that you cannot always have a good connection with everyone, even if you try all the techniques. Sometimes, you will encounter people who are simply difficult to get along with, and the best thing that you can do would be to leave them as they are and just move on. After all, there is no limit to your social circle. You can always expand it and meet new and interesting people with whom you can enjoy life.

- Casual talk

Learn to engage in casual conversations. When there is an opportunity, do not hesitate to ask another: "How are you?" This simple question can lead to all sorts of interesting talks. In fact, it can even create a wonderful relationship.

Casual talks usually take the form of shallow conversations. They are the everyday conversations that you encounter. Although they are often ignored or neglected, it does not change the fact that these casual talks create a connection. Now, it is up to you how you make use of this connection. Engaging in small talks or casual talks is usually the next step after being approachable. If you come to think of it, most relationships start from having small talks. Again, when you engage in a casual conversation, do not think of it as a little or unimportant conversation. Instead, you should look beyond it and appreciate the value that it brings. When you engage in any conversation, regardless if it is just a casual or small talk, a connection is made, and this connection can grow or diminish depending on what you do with it. Of course, just like any other relationship, it is always a two-way process. You cannot impose yourself on other people just as they cannot also impose themselves on you.

Any moment is an opportunity to engage in a casual conversation. Hence, any moment is a way to connect with another, and so there is a chance to improve or expand your social circle. Especially these days, technology has made it much simpler to connect with people. You can just use your mobile phone and send a message to another. Of course, this does not mean that you should rely on technology. Real connections and relationships should still be made in person, face to face. Still, technology is a useful tool that you can take advantage of to connect with people.

When you engage in a casual talk, it is a good advice not to be serious about it. Instead, learn to laugh and make jokes. A casual conversation should be light and easy. Do not make it difficult for people to talk to you. It is the time to be comfortable with each other. Hence, when you are engaged in a casual talk, avoid being serious. Just enjoy the company of another.

It should also be made clear that a small talk is not a meaningless conversation. It will only be meaningless if you make it so. However, if you know how to take advantage of a small talk, then you can develop it and even use it to create a lasting friendship with another. Hence, do not underestimate the power of small talks. Do not forget that most good relationships started out as small talks. So, the next time that you engage in any casual conversation, appreciate its value and use it to form a lasting relationship with another person. Of course, you are not forced to develop a conversation just to form a good relationship. You are also free to choose the people with whom you want to associate with — and a good way to get to know people better is by engaging in a casual conversation.

- Give compliments

This is a really important advice. Learn to give honest and positive compliments. Compliments express appreciation, and people love to be appreciated for who they are and what they do. Unfortunately, in today's world, so many people focus too much on themselves that they fail to give compliments to others. Giving compliments is an excellent way to win new friends and even influence people and make them want to know you better.

A common mistake when giving a compliment is not to mean what you are saying. Take note that in giving compliments, it is important for you to be sincere and mean what you are saying. Even if you say something nice, if the other person feels that you do not really mean what you are saying but only do so for the sake of giving a compliment, then it would not be much appreciated. In fact, it may even be taken as an offense.

The next time that you interact with someone, notice him and find something that you can comment on. Is there something good about him that you can say something nice about? As a rule, there is always something good that you can say about a person. The only thing that you need to do is to recognize it and tell it to him. Unfortunately, there are people who will only compliment you if you first say something nice about them. Do not wait for others to praise you. Be the gentleman and take the initiative.

You do not have to say something grand or remarkable. A good comment on one's outfit is also good enough. The important thing is to express your appreciation or admiration. You also do not have to make it a big deal. Just mention it to the person, but make sure that you do it sincerely. Otherwise, he might think that you are only making fun of him or mocking him.

When you say nice things about people, chances are that they will also say nice things about you. This another way to build a good relationship. As a rule, you should never say bad things about people, and never spread or participate in any gossip.

There is a pleasant feeling when you know that a person appreciates you. Although giving compliments is actually an easy thing to do, it is unfortunate that only a few people can do it well. It is good to make some form of self-examination. Ask yourself: When was the last time that I said something nice to someone and expressed my appreciation? The next question is: How often do I give compliments? Be honest with yourself. If you realize that you have become too focused on yourself that you fail to appreciate others, then now is the time to make some positive changes in your life. Do not be hard on yourself. The important thing is to be willing to be a better person, and the techniques/strategies in this book will help you do that.

- Ask questions

Ask questions. This is a good way to learn more about a person and establish a connection. Asking questions also encourage a person to open up to you. It is easy to ask questions, especially during the conversation. The key is to use it as a way to help the other person to express himself. Asking responsive questions is only about following the other person's train of thoughts and use follow up questions to help him express and explain his point. Of course, it also helps for you to better understand a person. Needless to say, after asking your questions, then you should also be ready to listen.

You need to learn to ask the right questions. Just as answers should be responsive to the questions being asked, the questions should also be responsive or relevant to what the other person is telling you. Although most people ask questions to understand what the other person is saying, do not forget that another useful application of asking questions is to help the other person express himself. By asking the right questions, you can make the conversation more comfortable for the other person.

Although there is no such thing as a wrong question, there is such thing as an effective question. Such kind of question develops the conversation. For example, if a person tells you that he is feeling sad, you can ask what it is that is making him sad, as well as what you can do to make him feel any better. As you can see, by asking the right questions, you can deepen the level of conversation and make it more meaningful.

However, do not let the conversation just be full of questions. You should, from time to time, give your own insights. If you cannot give your own insights, then at least give your own opinions on the matter, even if such opinions be completely based on what the other person has already told you.

The art of asking questions that can develop the conversation is an important element of effective communication. Of course, for you to be able to ask such kind of questions, you must learn to listen and understand the other person. A common mistake which prevents many people from asking the right questions is to judge and have wrong perceptions of others. When this happens, they fail to ask the right questions and start barking at the wrong tree. When you socialize, remember that it is important for you to be open and not to judge anyone.

If you want to improve your social life or simply want to develop any conversation, you will find that learning to ask effective questions can be truly helpful. Just like other skills in communication, this also takes time and practice to master.

- Positive thoughts

There is a teaching that says, "The happiness of your life depends upon the quality of your thoughts." Indeed, this is how powerful your thoughts are. If you keep positive and happy thoughts, chances are that you will have a happy life. However, if you harbor negative thoughts like hate and disappointments, then chances are that you will be sad in life.

People tend to be drawn to those who have a positive nature. If you have positive thoughts, then you are a positive person. If you are a positive person, you can easily attract people.

However, it should be noted that being positive means so much more than having positive thoughts. After all, how can you have positive thoughts in the first place? A key element is to have the right understanding. This has more to do with having self-realization than being too concerned about other people. Although building a social life primarily concerns other people, what people do not realize is that when you build a social life, the most important element or factor is yourself. If you improve yourself, then people tend to be more drawn to you. Consider, for example, a beautiful woman. Many people would want to get to know her and be connected to her. Of course, building a social life is not limited to physical attributes. You can also command attention and interest through other means, such as your attitude, accomplishments, and behavior, among others. This gives you many opportunities to connect with people.

Mid-Term Strategies

- Follow up and connect

By the time you reach this point, it is assumed that you were able to create a good relationship. However, even a good relationship does not guarantee anything. Indeed, even a good relationship can end quickly if you do not take care of it. Hence, there are certain things that you can do to protect and grow your relationship. One of which is to follow up and continue to connect with your current network. Just because you have spent a fine day with some friends does not mean that it already guarantees your relationship to last. Any kind of relationship is just like growing a plant. You have to water it on a regular basis. In the same way, you should also keep in touch with your circle from time to time. If you want to take care of certain people in your circle, then you should invest time in them. Be sure to contact and talk to them every now and then. It does not have to be on a regular basis, but it is important that you establish your presence in their life. Indeed, in the modern world, it is fairly easy to get carried away and forget about your social connections. If you want a fun and meaningful social life, then you must take care of your social connections.

To follow up and connect means that you should keep in touch with your network of friends. Talk and meet with them every now and then. If they are not doing any action to improve the relationship, then do not hesitate to be the one to take the first step to re-establish a meaningful connection.

Time is also an important social element. Although not really a requirement, it still plays a useful role in a relationship. Indeed, the more time is invested in a relationship, the harder it would be for anyone to break it. Somehow, time adds value. However, this concept of *invested time* only applies if you can maintain the relationship. For this to happen, then you should keep the relationship going. Now, not all people will take the initiative not to allow a certain relationship from fading completely. In this case, do not hesitate to be the one to take the necessary steps to keep the relationship alive.

By making a follow-up and connecting with people, you can impress your presence in their life, and it also assures them that they are a part of your life. Not to mention, people also notice it when somebody tries to keep in touch with them. However, it is worth noting that you should not force any connection to happen. Let the other person decide if he would also want to build a relationship with you. Keep in mind that you can only encourage people to be a part of your social life, but you should not keep them in your circle if they ever want to leave. Building good relationships is a two-way process, and it should be made freely by the parties without any form of manipulation or control.

- Set meetings

To maintain and strengthen relationships, it is good to meet with people from time to time. Although you can easily connect with people through social media and the likes, personal or face-to-face meetings is still important. This is the best way to keep people in your circle. Once you lose touch with people, then they start to disappear from your social circle. Setting a meeting is also a good way to rekindle past relationships that have become dull or inactive.

A meeting does not have to be formal or luxurious. A simple lunch or dinner will do just fine. After all, the important thing is to get together and be able to connect with each other again.

How often should you set a meeting? Well, there is no hard and fast rule on this matter. The idea is to be able to keep in touch with each other again and maintain or even strengthen the relationship. This would depend on your schedule and how busy the other person is.

Do not feel bad if the other person cannot meet with you. The important thing is that you have invited him and that he is aware that you would like to spend time with him. After all, the modern world is full of busy people. Sometimes it is hard to get a free time to meet with friends. So, do not feel bad or discouraged if your offer gets turned down.

Of course, when people invite you to dinner or any meeting, it is good if you attend the said meeting. You should appreciate it when people make time just to be with you. In fact, appreciate the fact that a person has invited you because it means that he has not forgotten about you and would like to spend time with you.

So, what are you waiting for? It is time for you to examine your social circle and try to keep in touch with people in your circle. Meeting people, especially your trusted friends, can be fun and exciting.

- Do not be too sensitive

Although it is good to be sensitive, it is not a good idea to be overly sensitive. From time to time, you may encounter some bad jokes. If you are too sensitive, you can get easily offended to the point that you will think that the people around you have bad intentions and do not mean you well. Instead of being too sensitive, you should learn to laugh at jokes, even at yourself. However, take note that you should also not allow your kindness to be abused by others. If you notice that certain actions or words are deliberately made against you, then that is a different story. You should also learn to stand and defend yourself. However, you should do so respectfully. Otherwise, you will be just like those low-life people who are insecure about you. Remember never to step down to their level.

It is suggested that you should be sensitive when it comes to other people but a little insensitive when it comes to yourself. This way you can avoid hurting other people's feelings and not be hurt or offended by jokes. In a social situation, it is also unavoidable to have some misunderstandings. If you are too sensitive, then there may come a time when you can easily misinterpret certain gestures or words, which can make the situation complicated than it actually is. This is a kind of unnecessary stress, and you do not need to be bothered with such.

You should also realize that in a social setting, there are many things that are outside of your control. You cannot control what other people think or say about you. You should also accept a basic truth: You cannot please everyone. What this means is that no matter how you apply the techniques, there are simply those who would not want to form a bond or relationship with you. In fact, they might even criticize you. If this happens, do not be offended. Instead of feeling bad about yourself and other people, you should adapt a more positive attitude. Think positively and put your focus on positive things.

But, what if you get really offended? It is hard to ignore it when you feel that you are offended. So, in this case, what should you do? How can you complain without ruining the relationship? This is important for you to learn because, in the course of a relationship, you may sometimes feel offended. Additionally, you need to voice out how you feel to feel better. But, how do you go about doing it without risking your relationship? The key is not to complain but to explain yourself gently. Take note that you should be gentle. Do not use harsh words, and do not be mad. You should always have respect for other people. Keep in mind that you can always express yourself in a way that will not be offensive to others. So, just calm down and talk clearly and gently. Most of the time, people will understand why you feel offended and would even apologize to you. Unfortunately, some people are just thick-skinned and difficult to deal with. If they do not apologize despite how wrong they are, then consider it a blessing that now you know those people who are not really your friends. This will allow you not to waste more time with them. Instead, you can make better use of your time.

- Strengthen the relationship

You should always work on strengthening your relationship. Now, there are many ways to do this. In fact, the strategies in this book revolve around strengthening your relationships with people. Strong relationships create a happy and enjoyable social life. It should be noted that this should be a mutual effort. If you notice that the other person is not truly sincere and is not being true with you, then you would not have to continue to make time and efforts to strengthen the relationship. You would do much better if you invest the same energy with someone else.

Again, do not forget that a relationship should be mutual. It is a two-way process of giving and receiving. Hence, you should be careful about this. Otherwise, there is a risk that other people might simply take advantage of you.

Although your intention is good that you want to improve your existing relationship with people, you should also consider the fact that not everyone in your circle is good and kind. In fact, it is not uncommon to meet people who have the habit of abusing another person's kindness. It is best to stay away from such shallow and low-life people. Remind yourself that you have the right and freedom to choose those who will compose your inner circle.

If mutually made, strengthening a relationship is much worth it. In fact, it can be considered a fun and enjoyable process. This is because you do not have to do it alone. This naturally takes place when you meet someone whose company you enjoy and who also enjoys your company. Most of the time, you do not even have to apply any techniques, and the relationship with just "click." By then, you will just realize that you have earned a new friend whom you can trust.

- Be true

This is a very important advice. In everything that you do, be true. This means that you should be true to yourself and to other people. However, it should be noted that before you can be true to others, you must first be true to yourself. If you are not true to yourself, then you cannot project an honest social image.

It is being true to yourself where the real problem is. Unfortunately, there are so many people who do not know themselves anymore. They have been heavily influenced by the media and society that they have become a product of other people's thoughts. They live their life shaped by the expectations of others instead of how they truly want to live an honest and fulfilling life.

To be true to yourself, then you have to know yourself. Accept all of your strengths and embrace your weaknesses. Do your best to develop your strengths and overcome your weaknesses. A common problem is to keep a blind eye on your weaknesses. Again, it is important for you to know who you really are. Otherwise, you cannot be true to yourself and to others.

It is important that you should always be true, or else you would not be able to act sincerely. As you already know, sincerity is very important in forming a good and lasting relationship. Without sincerity, it would be hard to apply effectively all the techniques in this book. You should realize that building a good and enjoyable social life has more to do with yourself than other people. If you improve your personality and way of thinking, then you will realize that it is not difficult to build good relationships. As human beings, it is actually part of our nature to connect and interact with people, which include having healthy and enjoyable relationships.

- Build trust

All good relationships are based on trust. Without trust, it is impossible to have a meaningful relationship with anyone. Now, it should be noted that it takes time and effort to build trust, but it can only take a second to ruin it. Trust is a sensitive thing, and so you must take good care of it.

Building trust is just like building any good relationship. It is composed of many actions that are taken together. There are two common pitfalls that you should avoid: lying and revealing the secrets of another. These two flaws can completely break a person's trust, so never commit these things no matter what, even if you get into a fight with your friend. After all, after a fight, there is still a chance for reconciliation.

Building trust is mostly about being true. Be true in your words, as well as in your deeds. As long as you stick to the teachings in this book, then you will not find it hard to build trust. Now, a common problem is for this trust to be broken after months or years in a relationship. As humans, we tend to commit mistakes and blunders from time to time. Now, all other offenses can easily be forgivable. However, once you break a person's trust, then it becomes very serious. So, as much as possible, stay away from occasions and temptations that can lead you to break other people's trust in you.

You should pay attention to and protect your reputation. However, it should be noted that this does not mean that you should worry too much about what other people may think of you. You should realize that you cannot control the thoughts of other people, and they are free to think of you in any way that they want. As long as you are true to yourself and other people and handle all your affairs with honesty, then your conscience is clear — and this is what is important.

You do not need to prove to other people that you are worthy of their trust. After all, you do not socialize with other people to please them. Many people commit the mistake of thinking that to grow their circle, then they should continue to please others. The problem here is that if you follow this approach, you will end up being a different person from who you really are. You will become a person shaped by other people's expectations, and this would not make you a truly happy person. Instead, people should like you for who you are. You must be yourself. Socializing teaches you to know more about yourself and encourages you to be a better person. In fact, simply by improving yourself, you can already earn lots of friends. As people say, others are just a mirror of who you are. If you are a good person, then chances are that you will be surrounded by good people. As another saying goes, "Birds of the same feather flock together."

- Express appreciation

Expressing appreciation is another very important element in building a good relationship. Fortunately, this is very easy to do. Unfortunately, many people still fail to do it. If a person does something good to you, never forget to show your appreciation and say, "Thank you."

Another effective way to show your appreciation is by clearly telling a person that you appreciate what he has done to you. Although a person may not expect anything in return, it still gives him a pleasant feeling if he knows that his efforts are appreciated. Therefore, do not hesitate to express your appreciation whenever possible.

Another way to express appreciation is to do something nice to a person. It is important to note that you do this not to pay back the person but only to express your appreciation. If you do something nice to a person simply to pay back his kindness, that might even be interpreted by some as an insult. Rather, consider forming a mutual relationship with people.

- Offer a helping hand

One of the best ways to connect with another person is by offering a helping hand. When a person is in need of help, take the initiative to give some assistance. People do not usually forget those who have helped them in a time of need. In fact, this is also how many meaningful bonds are formed. As you continue to get along in your relationship with people, there will come a time that someone in your circle may need some help. Do not be like the others who just hope that another person would extend a helping hand. Rather, be the one to take positive actions and help the one in need.

This is also an opportunity to show your good side. Helping people is definitely positive in nature and keeps you in a positive light. However, do not be like the others who lack sincerity in what they do. When you help people, you should help them with all your heart. Never exercise any half-hearted affection. Hence, if you honestly do not feel like extending help to someone, then it is better for you not to help out than be a hypocrite. Again, sincerity is very important in any relationship.

Normally, during the time that you are helping a person, the bond is strengthened. However, take note that just like any other act of love, there is also a risk involved when you help someone. Although most people would express their appreciation, there are those who might not even be grateful for your help. Instead of feeling bad because of such people, just be content that you have helped someone and that you have been a good person.

- Communicate effectively

It is a common knowledge that effective communication is important in any relationship. In fact, poor communication usually leads to a bad relationship. Indeed, having misunderstandings is a common reason why some relationships do not last. Hence, it is essential that you learn to communicate effectively.

When it comes to communication, you need to take note that it is a two-way process. This means that the parties must take turns between talking and listening. Just as you want to be heard and understood, you should also realize that other people want to be understood. This is why effective communication creates mutual relationships.

- Forgive

In a relationship, mistakes are bound to happen. After all, you are only human. Even if you are being very careful, you cannot prevent other people from committing mistakes. Hence, it is important for you to learn to forgive. Every now and then, someone from your circle may commit a fault against you. It is up to you to forgive other people's errors. If you do not know how to forgive, then you may not be able to have any lasting relationship. Even in an intimate husband and wife relationship, arguments and even some fights are normal. Similar things can arise in your social circle. This is why you must learn to forgive. Forgive but do not forget. If you forget about it, then you might fail to learn the lesson behind it.

Now, it is not always easy to extend forgiveness. You do not have to forgive right away especially if you do not feel it in your heart. Once you decide to be social, you should already expect that there will be times when you will have to exercise the virtue of forgiving.

- Make it enjoyable

Make your relationship as enjoyable as possible. In fact, the very reason why people want to connect and interact with one another is to improve the quality of their life. Hence, do not be too serious and learn to have fun. You should enjoy every moment that you spend with another. In fact, if you come to think of it, building a social life is actually a fun activity. You do not have to be so serious about it. It is not a workplace, so do not treat it like work. In fact, when you connect with nice people, chances are that you would even enjoy it. After all, people usually connect with others to relax and just have fun. Make every meeting as enjoyable as possible. However, you should also be sensitive enough. If you notice that the other person wants to be serious and talk about something, then you should also act appropriately.

Although this book shares effective techniques, know that a good way to create a pleasant relationship is to have fun with another. However, you should be careful about this. Just because a person is with you during times of pleasure does not mean that he will still be with you in times of problem. So, be careful with whom you trust. Indeed, it is not that easy to find a real friend these days. However, the good news is that it is still possible. When you open up your social circle and begin to reach out, you will definitely meet lots of different people, and some of these people might be the one who could make your life much happier and meaningful.

- Send a greeting

Be sure to send a greeting when there is a special occasion, especially if a person is celebrating his birthday. For this who are within his social circle, this is already considered as normal. Many people would appreciate such friendly gesture and could even invite you to the celebration of their special day. These days, it is very easy to send a greeting. You can easily send them a message or even call their mobile phone. If you want, you can also buy them a gift and have it delivered to their doorstep. You have many options to express your appreciation and to extend a greeting to another.

- Share insights

Feel free to share your insights with people. This is a good way to express your thoughts about something. If a person likes your way of thinking, then there is a good chance that the conversation can develop a good relationship. Hence, this is an effective way of growing your social circle. Now, it should be noted that you should be careful with the insights that you share. As a suggestion, only share your insights if you think that you have something nice or good to say. If you are not sure of your insights, then it is better to just keep quiet and let other people do the talking. As a rule, you should use your words carefully and wisely. If you do not have something good to say, then be silent. Also, giving meaningless or shallow insights can create a negative impression of yourself.

- Do not argue

You should avoid all arguments. The truth is that nobody really wins an argument. Even if you lay down good and impressive reasons to support your case, you will only manage to injure the pride of another person. This is why nobody wins an argument. You may, technically, win an argument, but then you would lose a friend or at least a potential friend. After all, you are not in a court of law where a judge would decide the winner. Instead of arguing, you should explain your thoughts and ideas in a respectful manner without being adverse to anyone. The best way is just to be honest and gentle at the same time. Do not use foul or offensive language, and always express yourself nicely.

Now, there are people who may want to get into an argument with you. Unfortunately, there are simply people who want to boast about their intelligence without realizing that it only makes them more foolish. If ever you encounter such kind of person, remind yourself that you do not need to argue with you, even if you feel tempted to do so. Otherwise, you will end up just like him. The better and suggested approach is for you to just deliver your point nicely and do not argue with anyone. Getting into an argument is not good. If you lose, then obviously that is not good for you and will only make you look stupid. However, if you win, chances are that you have insulted or embarrassed another person. Therefore, avoid all kinds of arguments.

It should be noted that just because you share different or conflicting views does not always mean that you are already arguing with another. Arguments have more to do with the state of mind and the environment of the conversation. If it is adversarial, then it can be considered as an argument. However, there are also people who can talk about things in a creative or constructive manner. This is the type of conversation that is encouraging. In this kind of conversation, you can talk about the subject and even share different and even contradicting opinions with one another. However, this will depend upon the parties involved in a conversation whether they really have an open mind or not, as well as the quality of their intentions for engaging in the conversation.

Long-Term Strategies

- Continuous improvement

Just because your bond has already lasted for several years does not mean that you no longer have to give it any time and effort. In fact, this is one of the important moments when you should work on your relationship. By this time, you have already known one another so well, including all your strengths and weaknesses. You should always aim for continuous improvement. Always try to improve yourself and your relationship with people. A common mistake is to stay in one's comfort zone. Although many people tend to stay in their comfort zone, they are often the ones who usually miss out on wonderful opportunities to strengthen their relationships. It is unfortunate that only a few people have experienced a close and intimate bond with their friends. Sad to say, it is not that easy to find a real friend. Indeed, in a person's social circle, more than 90% of it would be composed of people you do not even trust completely.

Always strive for continuous improvement. Expand your circle as much as you want and fill it with good and positive people. Also, pay attention to your current network and find out ways on how you can further develop your relationship with the people in your network.

It is also noteworthy that continuous improvement does not just apply to your relationship with other people. In fact, this is more related to your own self. You should strive to be a better person. Do not forget that the more that you improve yourself, then it will be easier for you to attract people into your social circle. Of course, improving yourself does not come without challenges. In fact, the challenges can help you become a better person, depending on how you face them. The key is to be persistent and not give up. It is okay and normal to experience some failures. However, realize that you do not really fail and that you only fail when you stop trying. If you do not give up and continue to be a better person, then you can never be defeated, and there is so much for you to learn and gain.

Continuous improvement is a life-long journey. You should keep your enthusiasm alive. Although it is good to relax from time to time, do not get used to staying in your comfort zone. Life is full of lessons and experiences. Continue to improve your social life and enjoy a more meaningful life.

- Form a more powerful and meaningful bond of friendship

This kind of bond is quite rare but is nonetheless doable. Usually, it takes years for this to happen. So how do you form a more meaningful bond? Well, it is actually simpler than you might think. It is composed of the little things. Indeed, in a relationship, small things matter. And, if you add them up altogether, they can be one valuable and meaningful thing. A powerful and meaningful bond of friendship usually occurs on its own after years of being in a good relationship with people. Of course, you cannot expect to form this kind of bond with everyone in your social circle, but only with those whom you really trust. This is the kind of bond that is worth pursuing and fighting for. Unfortunately, it is not that easy to find or create. Since relationship is a two-way process, then the other person should also be good enough. Otherwise, problems may arise in the future. Still, this kind of bond is worth finding since it is one of the best bonds in the world where you know that whatever happens in life, you have someone who will stand by you no matter what happens.

You do not always have to look so far to find a person (or people) with whom you can have this kind of friendship. Sometimes people look for a perfect friend without realizing that such kind of friend does not exist since nobody is perfect. Sometimes the best of friends that you are looking for is already there in front of you. You just have to be more sensitive and considerate. However, if you are sure that you still do not have a network with whom to share this kind of friendship, then do not worry about it. Just be more open and soon enough you will find people whom you can trust and who will treat you right. When you find such people, it is strongly advised that you hold on to them, even fight for them, because such kind of people is rare to find.

- Stick to the "rules"

It is suggested that you stick to the rules or strategies in this book. If you try them for a few times and they do not seem to work, do not be discouraged. Indeed, many of the teachings in this book, although simple and easy to do, still take time and effort to be applied effectively. Just give yourself enough time and allow yourself to adjust. Once you get the hang of it, you will be able to perform these strategies effectively. Indeed, you should practice the techniques in this book until you get used to them to the point that they become a natural part of you.

It should be made clear that there are no strict rules when it comes to managing or improving one's social life. There are only suggestions and pieces of advice that you can listen to. Still, it is up to you to make your decision and take action as to what you believe is best. However, it should be noted that these "rules" as shared in this book have been proven effective for many years. Therefore, it is encouraged that you stick to the "rules" and learn. After some time, you will start to appreciate their real meaning.

But, how do you stick to the rules? Sticking to the rules simply means continuously applying the teachings in this book and learning from them. After some time, these teachings will be a normal part of you that it would take almost no effort for you to observe them. By that time, you will be able to realize their real meaning and importance.

Chapter 13: Best Practices

✓ Continuous practice

Even if you read all the books about building a social life, it would not turn you into a social magnet. When it comes to becoming a highly social person, it is the application of the teachings that matter the most. In fact, there are people who have not read any book on the subject of socializing but have a rich social life. Indeed, some people are naturally gifted with social skills. However, the good news is that these social skills or strategies are learnable. Of course, the first step is for you to know about them, so that you will know just what positive actions to do. Needless to say, this book has already provided you with the strategies that you need to learn. It is now just a matter of applying the strategies. So, it is time for you to put your knowledge into actual practice.

You may find some of the strategies in this book easy to do while others may take more time to learn. Do not worry, that is normal. After all, it is not that easy to learn a new skill. You have to give yourself enough time to adjust and learn the techniques. Not to mention, it also takes time and effort to reach a level of mastery whereby you no longer have to think of the strategies since they are already part of who you are. The important thing to do is to stick to your practice and persist in applying the techniques. After some time, you will get used to them and be able to use them without any effort. The important thing is not to give up and continue practicing the teachings.

✓ Make adjustments

The strategies in this book, just like in other books, should be taken only as a guide. They should not be taken so strictly as to limit you or prevent you from exercising your creative mind. Therefore, feel free to make any necessary adjustments that you might need. The important thing is that you understand the implications of the strategies and how you can use them to help build a good relationship. However, avoid making adjustments to the techniques in a way that will decrease their effectiveness.

You are also free to enhance the techniques if you can or even come up with your own unique ideas and strategies. After all, the art of socializing is not bound to any strict rules. Feel free to do what works for you. Sometimes you may have to do some trial and error, and that is normal. The important thing is that you continue to improve and learn. Experience can teach you a lot. Do not be content just by reading tips from books. Socializing is about having a real experience with people.

✓ Experiment

Feel free to experiment and develop your own techniques. Sometimes it is just a matter of trying what works for you. By the time that you finish reading this book and start practicing the techniques, you will surely realize other ways to improve or even develop your own approach. Do not allow yourself to be limited by this book. In fact, you should consider this book as an inspiration or encouragement to try out new things. After all, the art of socializing is a continuously evolving art.

It is good to reflect on the teachings in this book and find a deeper meaning. Also, think about your relationships with people and consider ways on how you can further improve them. Since you will be experimenting, it means that you should also be open to failures. It is a matter of trial and error. If an approach that you try fails, do not be discouraged. If you keep on trying, you will soon find an approach that works. It is a learning process. Also, even if an approach does not work, there is always a lesson that you can learn from it. As you can see, when you experiment, there is nothing for you to worry about but there is so much that you can gain.

Take it easy

Improving your social life should not be some kind of work. Although it also takes time and effort, you should not be too hard on yourself. You do not need to learn all of the techniques at once. Especially if you are just starting out, the suggested method is simply to choose one technique to learn and apply. Once you get used to it, then you can include another technique. You do not need to make it complicated. Keep things light and easy. After all, socializing should be fun. If it will just give you a difficult time, then why bother doing it? Again, do not be hard on yourself. If you commit mistakes, then stop for a while, think about it and learn from it, and then move on. Consider everything, including any mistakes that you may commit along the way, as part of the learning process that will teach you how to socialize more effectively and be a better person.

Do not think of the techniques in this book (and in other books or articles) as imposing rules and things that you must do. Rather, think of them as a way to improve yourself. You are free to apply them in your life at any time you want. You do not need to be hard on yourself. In fact, if you feel that socializing is about being hard on yourself and disciplining yourself severely, then you have a wrong understanding of what socializing is all about. If you are hard on yourself, then you are taking a wrong approach and perspective. Do not be pressured. The important thing is that you continuously try to improve yourself. Also, keep in mind that you do not have to be perfect just as you do not expect for other people to be perfect.

✓ Be sincere

Sincerity is important in any relationship. In fact, when you apply any of the techniques in this book, you should always exercise sincerity. This is not just applying the right techniques. You should be sincere in all your dealings with people. Keep in mind that in a social life, you get to deal with real people, and people have emotions. If a person finds out or even just feels that you are not sincere enough, then it will be difficult to gain his trust. In fact, if you are not sincere, even if you speak kind words, they would not sound as meaningful. Be sincere in everything that you do. Again, building a social life is not about pleasing other people. What you should realize is that it is more about improving yourself and becoming a better person.

Now, sincerity is not something that you can just force or impose upon yourself. This is actually what makes it challenging. Sincerity has to be genuine. The problem is that you cannot act it out or simply tell yourself that you are being sincere. Rather, you have to feel it in your heart. Unfortunately, many people have lost the sense of being sincere. Instead of being sincere, they look forward to being able to manipulate others. This is wrong because it makes a person to be less human. Instead of connecting with another human being, you will end up seeking superiority and a way to manipulate others. As you can see, the intention itself is no longer good. Hence, there is really no way for you to be sincere enough at all.

The key to becoming sincere comes from good intentions. It should come from a heart that seeks to be a better person. Before you can treat others sincerely, you should first learn to be sincere with yourself. Once you understand what sincerity really is, then you can extend that sincerity to other people. Sincerity is not a technique but a state of mind. It is not something that you can lie to yourself. For you to actually feel it, then you need to be it (be sincere).

A common hindrance to becoming sincere is one's personal interest, especially such interest that is geared to achieving your own personal gain. If you have a problem with being sincere, then a helpful tip is to stop thinking about yourself and start thinking about the other person. It is when you seek your own gain that you fail to be sincere. After all, you can still get what you want without having to sacrifice sincerity. The best approach is to be mutual in all things. Do not manipulate or deceive other people. It is okay and normal to think about yourself but also think about the good of other people. In a social situation, you must never resort to selfishness but should also consider what is good for others.

✓ Relax and have fun

Building a good and enjoyable social life should not give you a hard time. In fact, it should be fun and enjoyable. So, do not be pressured. Instead, you have to relax. The techniques in this book will also be easier to apply when you are relaxed. Socializing should be fun. If it is not fun, then you are probably not doing it right.

Sometimes it is not really your fault. There are times when even if you apply the teachings in this book, you will still not be able to build a relationship with someone. This is not really because of your fault. Sometimes it is just the connection is not as mutual as you would hope for. Do not worry, this is also normal. You cannot force people to be part of your social life just as they cannot force you to be a part of theirs. It is a free choice that people make. From time to time, you really have to say *no*, or accept it when people say *no*. When this happens, do not feel bad about it. Just relax and move on. Socializing should be made in a positive atmosphere, which should be fun and enjoyable.

If you are not happy being with certain people, then do not make things complicated. The best course of action would be to simply move to another circle. It is not about pleasing people or making others like you. If a connection does not work, then you can just abandon it and seek more meaningful and enjoyable connections.

Conclusion

Thanks for making it through to the end of this book. We hope it was informative and able to provide you with all of the tools you need to achieve your goals whatever they may be.

The next step is to apply everything that you have learned and start growing your social circle. The techniques in this book will help you form the relationship that you have always wanted. Take note that some of these techniques may require some practice to execute them effectively. The important thing is to do your best to become a better person and persist in practicing the techniques. Again, do not forget the importance of sincerity. Even if you apply all the techniques in this book, they would not have the same effect if you are not sincere with your intentions and actions. However, sincerity alone is not enough. Even if you are sincere, you also need to take positive actions to show or express your sincerity, and the best way to do that is by applying the techniques in this book.

Last but not least, you should understand that this book should not limit you in any way. Instead, you should use this book as a guide and let it inspire you to be good and to do good. After all, building good relationships with people is easy, especially if you are a good person.

Finally, if you found this book useful in any way, a review on Amazon is always appreciated!

CPSIA information can be obtained
at www.ICGtesting.com
Printed in the USA
BVHW091037100621
609274BV00002B/771